D1257909

SUPERWOMEN in STEM

Women Scientists in Math and Coding

CATHERINE BRERETON

Gareth Stevens
PUBLISHING

Please visit our website, www.garethstevens.com.
For a free color catalog of all our high-quality books,
call toll-free 1-800-542-2595 or fax 1-877-542-2596.

Cataloging-in-Publication Data

Names: Brereton, Catherine.
Title: Women scientists in math and coding / Catherine Brereton.
Description: New York : Gareth Stevens Publishing, 2018. | Series: Superwomen in STEM | Includes index.
Identifiers: LCCN ISBN 9781538214695 (pbk.) | ISBN 9781538214084 (library bound) | ISBN 9781538214701 (6 pack)
Subjects: LCSH: Women in science--Juvenile literature. | Women scientists--Juvenile literature. | Women in mathematics.
Classification: LCC Q141.B74 2018 | DDC 509.2'520973--dc23

Published in 2018 by
Gareth Stevens Publishing
111 East 14th Street, Suite 349
New York, NY 10003

For Brown Bear Books Ltd:
Text and Editor: Nancy Dickmann
Designer and Illustrator: Supriya Sahai
Editorial Director: Lindsey Lowe
Children's Publisher: Anne O'Daly
Design Manager: Keith Davis
Picture Manager: Sophie Mortimer
Concept development: Square and Circus / Brown Bear Books Ltd

Picture Credits: Cover: Illustrations of women: Supriya Sahai. All icons Shutterstock: Zabrotskaya Larysa, Mix3r, kotoffei, NaughtyNut, vasabii. Library of Congress: 21; NASA: 38, 39, 40, 41t, 41b; Public Domain: 9, 10, 11b, 33t, 20th Century Fox 5, Ada Lovelace Day/FindingAda 17b, Agnes Scott College 22, Alchetron.com 28, Bonhams 8, Computer History Museum 35, Flominator 20, Folger Shakespeare Library 4, GFDS CC-By-SA 16, Google Art Project/National Gallery of Scotland 15, Harvard University 33b, iq.intel.co.uk 27, Chris Nyborg 26, Smallbones 23, Smithsonian Institution 34, Karsten Sperling/spiff.de/photo 29, Sophiararebooks.com 17t, SSPL 14; Thinkstock: Photos.com 11t: United States Navy: 32.

Character artwork © Supriya Sahai
All other artwork Brown Bear Books Ltd

Brown Bear Books has made every attempt to contact the copyright holders.
If anyone has any information please contact licensing@brownbearbooks.co.uk

Manufactured in the United States of America

CPSIA compliance information: Batch #CW18GS. For further information contact Gareth Stevens, New York, New York at 1-800-542-2595.

Contents

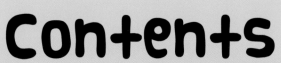

Making Sense of Math

Math is everywhere. When we think about numbers, quantities, and shapes in the world around us, we are thinking about math.

From the earliest times, people have counted and calculated, investigated the relationships between numbers, and examined forms and shapes in nature. The ancient Babylonians wrote multiplication tables and geometrical exercises in around 1900 BC. In the fourth century BC, Plato's Academy in Athens, ancient Greece, became the mathematical center of the world.

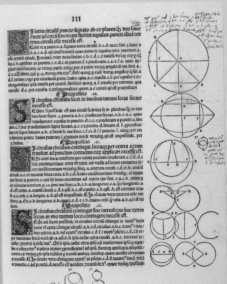

Euclid was an ancient Greek mathematician whose work has impact to this day. This is a medieval copy of his geometry book.

Katherine Johnson is a scientist who helped launch astronauts into space. Taraji P. Henson played her in the movie *Hidden Figures* (2016), above.

The work of ancient thinkers laid the foundations of math. These ideas are still taught today. Things really took off in the 1600s and 1700s, when many brilliant mathematicians were working. Isaac Newton and Gottfried Liebniz both invented theories of calculus, a branch of geometry that deals with how objects move and change. Some kinds of math are abstract, but math always has practical applications. Computer science grew out of the possibilities revealed by math. Coding is writing instructions for computers, and the instructions are written in mathematical language.

WOMEN IN MATH

Women have not always had the opportunity to study math, but where they have, they have excelled. The first woman mathematician, Hypatia, led the world of math way back in the 300s AD. Emmy Noether is considered to be one of the greatest mathematicians of all time. And it was a woman, Ada Lovelace, who invented the first computer program.

Hypatia
of Alexandria

Hypatia is the first known woman mathematician. She made great contributions to geometry and number theory and inspired future generations.

Hypatia was born around AD 370 in the city of Alexandria, Egypt, which at that time was part of the Byzantine (Roman) empire. Alexandria was known for being a great place of learning. Its library was the largest and most important in the ancient world, and scholarship and philosophy were central to city life. Hypatia's father, Theon, was a famous Greek scholar and mathematician, and the last known member of the Library of Alexandria.

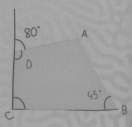

QUICK FACTS

NAME: Hypatia

BIRTH: AD c. 370,
Alexandria, Egypt (part of
the Byzantine empire)

OCCUPATION:
Mathematician, astronomer,
and philosopher

EDUCATION: Taught by her
father, Theon of Alexandria

STAR STUDENT

Theon made sure that his daughter grew up understanding their Greek culture and values, which included Greek teachings in math and astronomy. Hypatia became an expert in both. She overtook her father and made advancements in different areas of math. She became the leading mathematician of her time.

None of Hypatia's writings have survived, but she is mentioned in an ancient Byzantine encyclopedia called the Suda.

NEW LIGHT

Hypatia wrote reviews and explanations of her father's work, and also had her own insights into geometry and number theory. In geometry, she worked on ideas of parabolas, hyperbolas, and ellipses, which are all kinds of curves. In number theory, she wrote reviews of the work of an earlier mathematician, Diophantes of Alexandria. She also wrote many textbooks. Hypatia's thinking was greatly influenced by the classical Greek philosopher Plato (c. 428–348 BC), who had laid the foundations of western philosophy and science.

A portrait of Hypatia, painted in 1901.

Hypatia's work on geometry probably included writings about the different curves inside a cone.

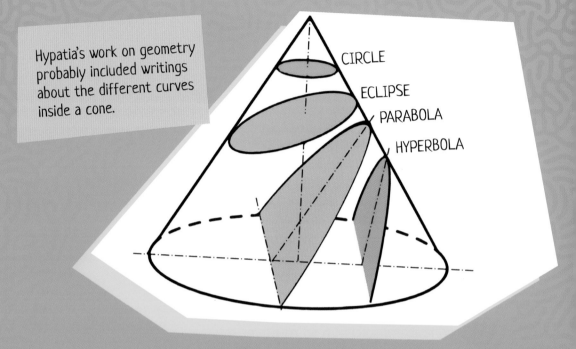

CIRCLE
ECLIPSE
PARABOLA
HYPERBOLA

As well as her work on math theories, Hypatia came up with practical innovations too. She invented a new kind of hydrometer, an instrument that measures the relative density of liquids. She may also have invented the astrolabe, a kind of astronomical calculator.

WISE WOMAN

It was very rare for women at that time to receive an education at all, let alone to reach such heights of learning. Yet Hypatia was admired and respected. She was one of Alexandria's first female teachers—she taught philosophy, following the ideas of Plato, as well as math. Known as "the Egyptian wise woman," she had many loyal students and always attracted large audiences to hear her lectures. People even traveled from far countries to hear her speak.

A 10-mile (16 km) wide crater on the moon is named for Hypatia.

THE SCHOOL OF ATHENS

The philosophers of ancient Greece are respected as some of the most important thinkers of all time. In the early 1500s, the Italian painter Raphael created a wall painting showing many figures of Greek learning. Plato and Aristotle are thought to be in the center, but there is no definite list telling us who everyone is. It is possible that Hypatia is in the scene. There is a story that Raphael originally put her in the middle of the painting, but church leaders told him to remove her—so he hid her out of the way!

Raphael's painting *School of Athens* (1509–1511).

66 **Revered Hypatia, ornament of learning, stainless star of wise teaching… I worship thee.** 99

Palladas,
Greek Anthology

RELIGIOUS TENSIONS

Hypatia lived at a time of tensions between Jews, Christians, and classical pagans (followers of classical gods and goddesses in ancient Greece and Rome). This unrest made it dangerous for pagans like Hypatia and her father to practice their traditions and customs, but perhaps it also made them all the more determined to keep classical learning alive.

The tensions would often turn violent. In AD 391, the Romans, who were by then Christian, outlawed paganism. Alexandria's great library had already suffered many acts of vandalism. Historians think that the library was finally destroyed in the violence of AD 391.

Hypatia met a horrible fate in AD 415. On her way home from teaching, she was dragged out of her chariot and beaten to death.

The violence became worse, and during one particularly bad episode in AD 415, Hypatia herself was a target. She was brutally killed in grisly fashion by a mob of Christian monks.

FEMINIST FIGUREHEAD

Hypatia's life and work, and her violent death, have made her a feminist symbol and a figurehead for the importance of learning in the face of ignorance, prejudice, and violence. Today, centuries after her life, many people see her as an inspiration.

Hypatia is admired today as an inspiring figurehead of learning.

Ada Lovelace

Ada Lovelace wrote the world's first computer program and was the first person to imagine what computers might one day be capable of.

Ada Lovelace make some truly remarkable contributions to computer science before computers even existed. She was born Ada Byron on December 10, 1815, in London, England. Ada was the daughter of a mathematician, Anne Isabella Milbanke, and the famous "mad, bad, and dangerous to know" romantic poet Lord Byron. Byron left the family when Ada was just a baby, and Ada's mother was eager to raise her to be nothing like her wild, irresponsible father.

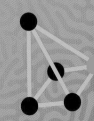

QUICK FACTS

....

NAME: born Augusta Ada Byron—her married name was Augusta Ada King, Countess of Lovelace, and she was known as Ada Lovelace

BIRTH: 1815, London, England

OCCUPATION: Mathematician

EDUCATION: Taught by private tutors

> 66 **The Analytical Engine weaves algebraical patterns just as [a loom] weaves flowers and leaves.** 99

HIGH-FLYING MATH STUDENT

Like most wealthy girls of the time, Ada was taught privately at home. However, unlike most wealthy girls, Ada's was a strict mathematical education. Her tutors were some of the best mathematicians of the day. She was often ill when she was a child, but this didn't stop her from studying and developing her love of science and math. At age 12, she became fascinated by flight. She studied the anatomy of birds, and drew up plans for a steam-powered flying machine. She wrote about her findings in a book called *Flyology*.

COMPUTER PIONEERS

In 1833, at age 17, Ada met the math professor and computing pioneer Charles Babbage. He was working on his Difference Engine, a machine that could perform math calculations. He never built a complete working version of the machine, but it is thought of as the first computer. Ada was excited by Babbage's invention

Ada Lovelace described herself as a "poetical scientist." She saw no division between art and science and knew that imagination and intuition are vital for a scientist.

14

MARY SOMERVILLE

A science writer, mathematician, and polymath (someone who excels in many fields of learning), Mary Somerville was part of a group of scientists and thinkers in London, England, in the 1800s. She was math tutor to Ada Lovelace and introduced her to Charles Babbage. Mary and astronomer Caroline Herschel were the first women to be nominated as members of the Royal Society, Britain's most important scientific institution.

Mary Somerville wrote about many math and science topics in a clear style.

and begged him to let her work with him. Although he said he was far too busy to take on a student, this didn't stop Ada.

ANALYTICAL ENGINE

Ada got married and had three children, but she hadn't forgotten about Charles Babbage's exciting work. In 1842, Ada saw a French article about Babbage's latest idea, called the Analytical Engine. To impress Babbage, she decided to translate it. Along with the translation Ada wrote a detailed set of notes explaining how the Analytical Engine worked, something that many other scientists had failed to grasp. She even noted how it was distinct from the Difference Engine. Babbage was impressed, and their work together began.

As a child, Ada suffered headaches that clouded her vision. She also had a bad case of measles. She was left so weak that she needed crutches to walk.

Charles Babbage nicknamed Ada the "Enchantress of Numbers."

THE FIRST COMPUTER PROGRAM

Ada's translation and explanation were impressive enough, but her notes didn't stop there. She also included a detailed method for using the Analytical Engine to calculate a sequence of numbers known as Bernoulli numbers. Although Babbage's machine had not even been built, Ada's method is recognized as the world's first computer program, making Ada the first computer programmer.

IMAGINATIVE LEAP

With her inventive mind, Ada saw something that Babbage didn't see. His inventions were about numbers and calculations. Ada realized that numbers might represent other things.

In 1991, scientists at the Science Museum in London, England, built the first complete model of Babbage's Difference Engine No. 2.

In fact, this is just what today's computers do — they change music, text, pictures, and sounds into numbers, and they use numbers to perform an amazing variety of functions. Ada was the first to imagine all this and to see just how powerful computers might one day become.

Ada died in 1852, and her brilliance only gained real recognition when Alan Turing, a British code-breaker and computing pioneer during World War II (1939–1945), said that her work had been his inspiration. The computer language "Ada" is named for her and used today.

This is Ada's "Note G," the set of instructions known as the world's first computer program.

ADA LOVELACE DAY

Since 2009, the second Tuesday in October is Ada Lovelace Day. This is a worldwide celebration of the achievements of women in science, technology, engineering, and math. Every year there are hundreds of events all over the world, encouraging girls to pursue their interest in these subjects.

Students visit an exhibition for Ada Lovelace Day at the world's biggest computer museum in Padeborg, Germany, in 2015.

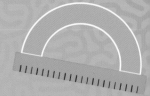

Emmy Noether

Mathematician Emmy Noether is celebrated as one of the most important mathematicians of the 1900s and possibly the greatest female mathematician ever.

Emmy Noether was born on March 23, 1882, in Erlangen, Germany. Her family was Jewish and her father was a math professor. Being a girl, she was encouraged to study French, English, and music. She excelled at all three subjects and gained the qualification needed to teach languages at girls' schools. But Emmy wanted to study math, and she decided to go instead to the University of Erlangen.

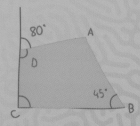

QUICK FACTS

NAME: Amalie Emmy Noether

BIRTH: 1882, Erlangen, Germany

OCCUPATION: Mathematician and physicist

EDUCATION: University of Erlangen

66 My [algebraic] methods are really methods of working and thinking; this is why they have crept in everywhere anonymously. **99**

A STRUGGLE TO STUDY

Going to university was a brave and unconventional step. Emmy was one of just two women among 986 students, and they were not allowed to join in fully. Emmy had to get permission from every professor whose classes she wanted to attend, and she had to sit at the back of class. In 1908, she started teaching at the university's Mathematical Institute, sometimes covering for her father if he was sick. Women were not officially allowed to teach, so she worked without pay or a job title for seven years.

It was obvious that Emmy was a brilliant mathematician. In 1915, she was invited to join the University of Göttingen, where she carried on her research and teaching. At first, she was not paid there, either.

This postcard shows the University of Erlangen in 1915, the year Emmy finished working there.

The famous physicist Albert Einstein had just published his Theory of General Relativity, and Emmy focused her research on the math behind this theory. Some colleagues objected to a woman professor, and she often had to work using a male professor's name.

ADVANCES IN ALGEBRA

Emmy had a very original mind, which allowed her to make new and exciting discoveries and connections. She made many important developments in a branch of math called abstract algebra. She came up with theorems about groups and rings, number fields, and much more. She headed a revolution in this field, and many of her students went on to make important contributions to the subject, too. Her work is the basis for much of today's pioneering research in physics.

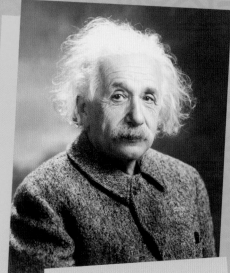

Physics and math genius Albert Einstein made some of the most important scientific discoveries ever.

THE NOETHER THEOREM

Emmy gave her name to her most famous theorem. It concerns the relationship between energy, time, and momentum. It says that whether you throw a ball in the air tomorrow or next week will have no effect on the ball's route through the air. The route will always be the same, as the universe uses the least amount of energy possible to get something done.

It seems working in an all-men environment didn't faze Emmy. In Göttingen, she also took up swimming at a men-only pool!

TEACHING

Some of Emmy's students made fun of her messy appearance and the fact she didn't care much for polite manners. They disliked the way her lectures could be unplanned and spontaneous. But she was popular with many students, who became known as "Noether boys." She was devoted to teaching. Once, when the university building was closed for a holiday, she took a group of students to a local coffee house and lectured there.

PERSECUTION AND EXILE

In 1933, Adolf Hitler came to power in Germany, and state persecution of Jewish people began. There were anti-Jewish protests at the university. In April 1933, Hitler's Nazi government fired most Jewish university professors, Emmy Noether included.

Emmy Noether faced sexism time and time again throughout her brilliant career — and also suffered persecution as a Jew.

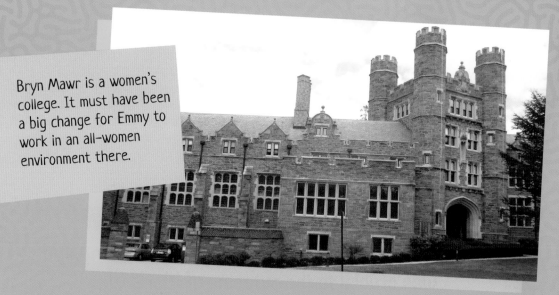

Bryn Mawr is a women's college. It must have been a big change for Emmy to work in an all-women environment there.

Emmy accepted this unjust decision calmly. She still thought of her students, inviting them to her home to discuss math and their plans for the future. But it was too dangerous for her to stay in Germany. In September, 1933, Albert Einstein helped her to get a job at Bryn Mawr college in Pennsylvania. Sadly, Emmy did not have long to enjoy her new life in America. She died in 1935 at the age of 53.

THE GENIUS'S GENIUS

Emmy Noether was widely recognized as a brilliant mathematician during her lifetime. However, she didn't get all the honors she really deserved. In 1932, she was a key speaker at the International Congress of Mathematics in Zürich, Switzerland. Many of her friends and colleagues were annoyed that she wasn't elected to the German Academy of Sciences. But possibly the world's most famous scientific genius, Albert Einstein, had called *her* a genius.

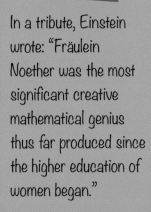

In a tribute, Einstein wrote: "Fräulein Noether was the most significant creative mathematical genius thus far produced since the higher education of women began."

The Bletchley Park
Code-Breakers

A top secret code-breaking operation in England was crucial to the outcome of World War II. Women made up 75 percent of its workforce.

I n wartime, military intelligence — knowing about the enemy's movements and plans—is just as important as any other aspect of fighting. When World War II broke out in August 1939, Britain immediately set up a listening and code-breaking operation, to find out about the German army's secrets. This intelligence may have shortened the war by around two years, saving thousands of lives. In a time when women's brainpower was undervalued, some super-smart women code-breakers helped to make the operation a success.

QUICK FACTS

NAME: The Bletchley Park
Code-Breakers

FORMED: 1938, Bletchley
Park, England

OCCUPATION: Code-breakers

CODE-BREAKING

Code-breaking, or cryptography, is a kind of puzzle-solving. The Germans were using Enigma machines to encrypt their messages (turn them into code), which made it nearly impossible to decode them. The British army recruited linguists (people who speak several languages), mathematicians, chess champions, and even crossword puzzle experts. They would have the thinking skills that might allow them to crack the near-unbreakable codes.

BLETCHLEY PARK

This top-secret code-breaking operation was set up at Bletchley Park, in the English countryside. The activity there was so secret that workers were told not to talk about it. Many just worked on their own piece of the jigsaw and didn't even know the significance of what they were doing themselves!

Bletchley Park intercepted and decoded hundreds of enemy air force messages and naval codes every day.

Hut 4 originally used for Naval intelligence.

Several huts were built at Bletchley. There were huts for each department, and a hut for refreshments and recreation.

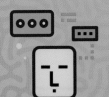

Dorothy du Boisson and Elsie Booker operate Colossus. The machine did not break the codes, but helped to speed up the process.

CRACKING CODED MESSAGES

Enemy communications were picked up by a chain of radio intercept stations. The messages were taken down on paper and sent to Bletchley Park. With amazing patience, the code-breakers would meticulously decrypt and analyze every message. When they had successfully decoded a message, the information was sent to government officials or military leaders.

HELP FROM COMPUTERS

The Bletchley Park code-breakers needed to speed up their efforts. One way of tackling this was to invent machines that could do some of the work. The Colossus machine, first used in 1944 and sometimes called the first computer, used punched paper tape containing possible solutions to a particular code. It cut the time used to crack codes from weeks to hours.

It was important that the enemy did not guess that people were trying to crack their codes. If they had suspected, they might have made the messages even more difficult to decode.

One of Joan Clarke's tasks was to decipher messages from enemy ships heading toward Allied troop and supply ships in time for the enemy to be stopped.

WOMEN AT WORK

Around 7,500 of the 10,000 people working at Bletchley Park, roughly 75 percent, were women. Most were young math graduates, German speakers, or just women who were good at puzzles! Most of the women were employed to do secretarial tasks. However, some worked on engineering and programming Colossus and other machines, and a select few worked as cryptographers—the top code-breaking job.

FOUR AMONG A FEW

Four women code-breakers were Ruth Briggs, Joan Clarke, Mavis Leaver, and Margaret Rock. Ruth was a cryptographer and translated decoded messages from German. Mathematician Joan is known for her work with Alan Turing, the mathematician, code-breaker, and computing pioneer, on cracking Enigma codes. Mavis and Margaret made the first breakthrough into discovering the Italian Navy's plans. That gave the Allies an advantage in the run-up to D-Day, which was a turning point in the war in 1941.

Joan Clarke became Deputy Head of Hut 8 in 1944. She had to crack codes in real time, and her work saved thousands of lives.

ENIGMA MACHINE

Enigma operators typed a message into the machine and it mechanically encrypted the letters. The person receiving the message needed to know what settings had been used, and then they could unscramble the message. The Bletchley Park code-breakers had to do this without knowing the settings. It was very difficult work. Alan Turing, one of the top Enigma code-breakers, figured out several techniques to break the codes.

wheels

An Enigma machine with three wheels. The receiver needed to know how the wheels were set.

INDUSTRIAL INTELLIGENCE

At Bletchley Park, code-breaking was carried out on an industrial scale. This was the birth of the information age. Alan Turing invented the idea of a "Universal Machine" that would decode and perform any set of instructions, instead of just one set, like Colossus did. Later, Turing would turn this into a practical plan for a computer—one of the first.

After the war ended in 1945, the code-breakers went back to their ordinary lives. It was not until the 1970s that people were allowed to say anything about the code-breaking operation at Bletchley Park. Finally, their vitally important contributions to the war effort received the recognition they deserved.

It was not until the 1970s that the British spoke about the race to crack Enigma. Colossus was even smashed up at the end of the war.

Grace Hopper

Nicknamed "Amazing Grace" and "Grandma COBOL," Grace Hopper was a pioneer who made it possible for anyone to learn to code.

G race Murray was born on December 9, 1906, in New York City. From a young age she was full of curiosity. At age seven, she decided to take apart all the alarm clocks in the house to figure out how they worked! Luckily, her parents encouraged her interests and her education, and she went on to study math and physics at university. Grace gained her PhD in 1934 and took up a teaching position at Vassar College.

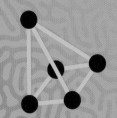

QUICK FACTS

NAME: Grace Murray Hopper

BIRTH: 1906, New York City, New York

OCCUPATION: Navy admiral, computer scientist

EDUCATION: Vassar College, Yale University

31

66 **A ship in port is safe; but that is not what ships are built for. Sail out to sea and do new things.** 99

MAKING HER MARK

In 1943, during World War II, Grace enlisted in the US Naval Reserve. She was sent to Harvard and joined a team programming one of the first-ever electronic computers, the Mark I. She could hardly wait to get her hands on this exciting new gadget, and figure it out as she had done with the alarm clocks.

The Mark I was the first machine that could do long calculations automatically. Before that, large groups of people known as "human calculators" or "human computers" did complex math by hand. Now a machine could do this, but first programmers needed to write programs that would tell the machine what calculations to do. Grace encouraged her small team of programmers to share common parts of programs. This reduced errors and cut down on the duplication of work.

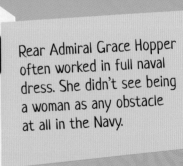

Rear Admiral Grace Hopper often worked in full naval dress. She didn't see being a woman as any obstacle at all in the Navy.

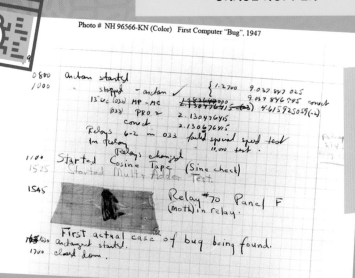

Photo # NH 96566-KN (Color) First Computer "Bug", 1947

Grace popularized the term "debugging" for fixing errors in code. She had to literally debug the Mark II computer when this moth got stuck in it!

Grace wrote the first computer manual—a 500-page history of the Mark I and guide to programming it.

VITAL WAR ROLE

Grace's team used the Mark I to solve problems that would help the war effort. These included equations for the Manhattan Project, the research effort that led to the development of the atomic bomb. She solved a very difficult calculation that was key to making the bomb explode properly.

MARK I

The Mark I computer was built from switches, relays, rotating shafts, and clutches. It had 750,000 electrical components and hundreds of miles of wire. It was huge: 51 feet (15.5 m) long, 8 feet (2.4 m) high and weighed over 10,000 pounds (4,500 kg)!

The Mark I's designer, Howard Aiken, was inspired by Babbage's Difference Engine.

"Humans are allergic to change. They love to say, 'We've always done it this way.' I try to fight that. That's why I have a clock on my wall that runs counterclockwise. "

UNIVERSAL COMPUTER LANGUAGE

Grace was always questioning things, and loved to discover new ways of solving problems. After the war, she stayed at Harvard as a Navy research fellow. She wanted to figure out a more "human" way of programming computers, one that would be easier for people to understand.

In the 1940s, you needed an advanced math degree to program computers. Binary code (0s and 1s) was used to program. Grace thought it would be much better if you could use real words to "talk" to computers. People said it was impossible, but she found a way to do it. In 1952 Grace invented the first compiler.

Grace wrote a program for the UNIVAC computer (shown here) that used words instead of numbers for instructions.

The compiler is a program that translates code from one computer language into another. Then Grace helped create COBOL, the first universal computer language. Today, programmers mostly use "if/thens" instead of 0s and 1s. Thanks to Grace, anyone can learn to code!

ROLL OF HONOR

Grace didn't stop there. After retirement, she eagerly took part in teaching young people. Grace received many honors for her incredible work. She was awarded the Society of Women Engineers' highest honor and was the first-ever winner of Computer Science "Man of the Year" Award. She also has a Navy ship, *USS Hopper*, named for her. She died in 1992, but in 2016 she was awarded the Presidential Medal of Freedom.

Grace had a pirate flag in her office, to remind people that sometimes you have to go against the system and do things differently.

JEAN JENNINGS BARTIK

Software pioneer Jean Jennings Bartik is known for her work on ENIAC, the world's first all-electronic (rather than electro-mechanical) computer, completed in 1946. Jean was hired fresh out of college by the US army, and was picked to program ENIAC, which was 1,000 times faster than any previous computer. There were no manuals, so she and her colleagues quizzed the engineers who had built ENIAC, and figured out what to do. They developed subroutines, nesting, and other basic programming techniques.

Jean Jennings Bartik was one of the first computer programmers.

Katherine Johnson

Katherine Johnson is an American math genius who reached for the stars. Her calculations helped to propel astronauts into space.

Katherine Johnson helped launch astronauts into space and was a trailblazer for African American women in science. Katherine Coleman was born on August 26, 1918, in a small town in West Virginia. From an early age she loved to count, and it was clear that she had an exceptional gift for math. In her town there was no school for African American children beyond eighth grade, so when Katherine was age 10, her family moved 120 miles (193 km) so she could continue her education.

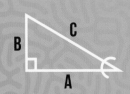

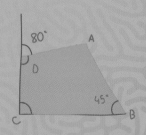

QUICK FACTS

NAME: Katherine Coleman Goble Johnson (born Katherine Coleman, she married first James Goble and later James Johnson)

BIRTH: 1918, White Sulphur Springs, West Virginia

OCCUPATION: Mathematician, physicist

EDUCATION: West Virginia State University, West Virginia University

> **I counted everything: the steps, the dishes, the stars in the sky.**

RACING AHEAD

Katherine graduated high school at just 14, and enrolled at a university, where she was a star student. She graduated at age 18, and was a teacher for a while before getting married and focusing on family life.

A HUMAN COMPUTER

In the 1950s, Katherine heard that NACA (later called NASA) was hiring African American women as "computers." These were mathematicians, usually women, who solved complicated math problems by hand, supporting NASA's engineers. Katherine joined a large pool of African American women "computers."

At NASA in 1962, Katherine's tools included a "celestial training device" with key coordinates for navigating in space.

REACHING INTO SPACE

This was the time of the Space Race—a rivalry between the United States and the Soviet Union to control space technology. From 1958, NASA worked tirelessly to put an astronaut into space. Figuring out how to do this—and how to return them safely—was a huge task. It required clever engineering and complex geometry calculations. As the project details developed, calculations had to be done and redone over and over. Katherine was key to this effort. She was especially brilliant at geometry, and with her skill, she calculated the flight paths the spacecraft would take, and the launch window. She calculated the flight path for the first American in space, Alan Shepard, in 1961.

Due to racial discrimincation, the African American women "computers" at NASA had to work, eat, and use bathrooms apart from their white colleagues.

MARY JACKSON

Mary Jackson worked in the computing pool at NASA at the same time as Katherine Johnson. Mary was chosen to work on a machine that recreated the wind conditions spacecraft would need to survive. She wanted to become an engineer herself, which took great determination. There were few woman engineers, and the nearest engineering school was whites-only. Mary went to court to get special permission to attend.

Mary Jackson at work as a NASA engineer in 1980.

GETTING AHEAD

Katherine pushed aside the obstacles of her race and gender. For a long time the only bathroom she was allowed to use was a 20-minute walk away from her desk, yet she said she didn't feel the segregation—everyone just got on with their work. She needed to fight for respect as a woman. She insisted on being allowed into top-level meetings, and she was the first woman to have her name as coauthor of a NASA report.

In 2017, 98-year-old Katherine appeared onstage at the Academy Awards alongside the stars of the hit movie *Hidden Figures*, which tells her story, along with those of Mary Jackson and Dorothy Vaughan.

AN ASTRONAUT ASKS FOR KATHERINE

In the days just before astronaut John Glenn was due to fly into space for the first piloted orbit of the Earth, a question came up. The new NASA mechanical computers came up with different results on different days when calculating details of the flight. Glenn asked for Katherine to check the math.

Astronaut John Glenn enters the *Friendship* space capsule that would take him on the *Mercury* mission to orbit the Earth.

Glenn only felt safe to go after Katherine checked the math. On February 20, 1962, Glenn orbited the Earth three times and returned safely. The mission was a success.

TO THE MOON

There were more successes to come for NASA and for Katherine. In 1969, NASA sent astronauts to the Moon, and Katherine calculated the flight paths that got them there. She worked for NASA for 33 years, contributing to space shuttle missions and to the plans for a Mars mission. Katherine has received many honors for her work.

Katherine receives the Presidential Medal of Freedom from President Obama in 2015.

DOROTHY VAUGHAN

Dorothy Vaughan was the first African American supervisor at NASA. She led the computing pool. When mechanical computers were first used at NASA, Dorothy decided to learn how to program them and began to teach her staff this new skill. Instead of losing their jobs when NASA switched over to mechanical computers, Dorothy and her staff became programming experts.

Math and computing trailblazer Dorothy Vaughan.

Timeline

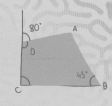

AD c. 370-415	Hypatia of Alexandria is the world's first-known woman mathematician.
1750	Émilie du Châtelet's French translation of Isaac Newton's *Principia Mathematica* is published.
1759	Maria Agnesi becomes professor of mathematics at the University of Bologna, Italy.
1800s	Sophie Germain works on her proof that is a step toward proving Fermat's Last Theorem.
1835	Mary Somerville and Caroline Herschel are nominated to become members of Britain's Royal Astronomical Society.
1842	Ada Lovelace writes the notes that are considered to be the first computer program.
1889	Sofia Kovalevskaya becomes the first full professor at a European university in modern times.
1915	Emmy Noether joins the University of Göttingen, where she carries out years of groundbreaking research in algebra.
1939-1945	World War II. In Britain, 75,000 women are part of the huge code-breaking operation at Bletchley Park. In the US, women mathematicians work on complex calculations that help in the development of new weapons. Women are at the forefront of the new science of computer programming.
1944	Grace Hopper starts programming the Mark I computer.
1946	An all-women team including Jean Jennings Bartik programs ENIAC, the first all-electronic computer.

1955-1972	In the Space Race, the United States and the Soviet Union compete to be the first to send an astronaut to space, the first to orbit the Earth, and the first to visit the Moon.
1958	Mary Jackson becomes the first black woman to be an engineer at NASA. Dorothy Vaughan leads a new, pioneering NASA team of computer programmers.
1959	Grace Hopper helps create the computer programming language COBOL.
1962	John Glenn is the first man to orbit the Earth. Katherine Johnson's calculations are crucial in getting him there.
1969	The US *Apollo 11* spaceflight lands astronauts on the Moon. Margaret Hamilton's software design and Katherine Johnson's flight path calculations are part of the achievement. Mary Jackson is one of the engineers who help develop the spacecraft.
1978	Carol Shaw starts work at video game company Atari.
1990	Tim Berners-Lee develops HTML, giving rise to the World Wide Web.
1994	Maryam Mirzakhani wins a gold medal at the International Mathematical Olympiad. Later (in 2014) she wins the world's top math prize, the Fields Medal.
2009	The first Ada Lovelace Day takes place.
2012	Shaffi Goldwasser wins the Turing Award for her work on cryptography.
2015-2016	Mathematicians Margaret Hamilton, Grace Hopper, and Katherine Johnson are awarded the Presidential Medal of Freedom.

Gallery

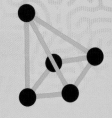

The scientists covered in this book are only a few of the women who have advanced the study of math and coding, but here are more who achieved great things.

MARIA AGNESI (1718-1799)

Author of the first book on calculus (a branch of math), Maria impressed the Pope so much that he appointed her to be professor of mathematics at the University of Bologna, Italy, in 1750. This made her the world's first woman university math professor.

MARIE-SOPHIE GERMAIN (1776-1831)

Staying indoors for her own safety during the French Revolution, Sophie turned to her father's library and found an interest in math. She discovered a proof that led to the proof of Fermat's Last Theorem—the greatest breakthrough in number theory until the 1960s. A type of prime number, the Sophie Germain prime, is named for her.

MARY LUCY CARTWRIGHT (1900-1998)

The first woman mathematician Fellow of the Royal Society, Mary worked during World War II on top-secret technology that became known as radar. She examined radio waves and came up with equations to explain the sometimes unstable way they behave. Her work was the beginning of the field of chaos theory.

MARGARET HAMILTON (born 1936)

A software design pioneer, Margaret was part of the team that designed in-flight systems for the first manned Moon mission. The designers were figuring everything out from scratch. Their creations included components such as error detection systems and recovery software.

CAROL SHAW (born 1955)

Known for being the first woman video game designer, Carol first became interested in computers—and computer games—in high school. Back then, kids didn't have computers at home! With a master's degree in computer science, she worked for the game company Atari and wrote games in the 1970s and 1980s.

SHAFFI GOLDWASSER (born 1958)

MIT professor Shaffi's papers have given rise to whole branches of computer science. She has made many contributions to cryptography and won the 2012 Turing Award for her work in this area.

MARYAM MIRZAKHANI (1977-2017)

The first woman to win the Fields Medal (the world's top math prize), Maryam was one of the first girls on Iran's International Mathematical Olympiad Team in 1994. Later she specialized in twisting and stretching surfaces. She died of cancer, aged just 40.

SCIENCE NOW

Today's mathematicians are working in every area you can think of—from figuring out the best way to program traffic lights and improving the way we predict earthquakes to developing new cyber security systems to keep ahead of hackers. It's not all serious—they're designing better games, too.

The women in this book were pioneers, working in a world dominated by men. Today, there are thousands of women in math, and many exciting things to be discovered!

What interests you most about math and coding? Would you like to write programs that will improve how calculations are done, or would you like to design computer games? Find out whether there are any events near you next Ada Lovelace Day, and visit STEM websites online to learn more.

Glossary

Allies The name given to the US, Britain, and others fighting on their side in World War II, including France, Canada, Poland, and the Soviet Union.

atomic bomb A bomb in which the explosive power is caused by the release of energy from splitting atoms, also called a nuclear bomb.

binary code A number system that uses just 0s and 1s.

D-Day An invasion of occupied France by American, Canadian, and British forces in June, 1944, which was a turning point in World War II.

feminism The belief that people of all genders should have the same rights and opportunities, and the effort to make this happen.

flight path The path made in air or space by something such as a spacecraft or airplane.

geometry A branch of math that deals with points, lines, angles, surfaces, and solids.

launch window The period of time in which a spacecraft must be launched for it to reach its target.

momentum Strength or force gained by moving.

NASA The National Aeronautics and Space Administration, a US organization responsible for space research.

orbit To travel in a circle around something, especially in space.

persecution Cruel or unfair treatment.

posthumously Happening to someone after they have died.

prime number Any whole number other than 0, 1, or -1 that can only be divided by itself and 1.

segregation Separation based on a category such as race.

sexism Unfair treatment based on gender, usually against women.

software The programs and other information used by a computer that make it carry out functions.

Soviet Union A large, powerful, country made up of many countries and centered on modern-day Russia, that existed from 1922 through 1991.

spontaneous Happening without any outside force or cause.

theorem A formula or statement in math.

Further Information

Books

Bodden, Valerie. *Programming Pioneer Ada Lovelace (STEM Trailblazer Bios)*. Lerner, 2016.

Doyle, Caitlin. *Girls Can Do Anything*. Firefly Books, 2016.

Patel, Mukul. *We've Got Your Number: Why Everything in the Universe is Numbers ... Including You*. Kingfisher, 2013.

Shetterley, Margot Lee. *Hidden Figures (Young Readers' Edition)*. HarperCollins, 2016.

Wallmark, Laurie. *Grace Hopper: Queen of Computer Code*. Sterling Children's Books, 2017.

Websites

Explore the timeline of computers here!
http://www.computerhistory.org/timeline/

Try out coding at this interactive site.
http://lightbot.com/

Learn more about STEM at this awesome site.
www.stemcenterusa.com

Publisher's note to educators and parents: Our editors have carefully reviewed these websites to ensure that they are suitable for students. Many websites change frequently, however, and we cannot guarantee that a site's future contents will continue to meet our high standards of quality and educational value. Be advised that students should be closely supervised whenever they access the Internet.

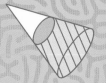

Index